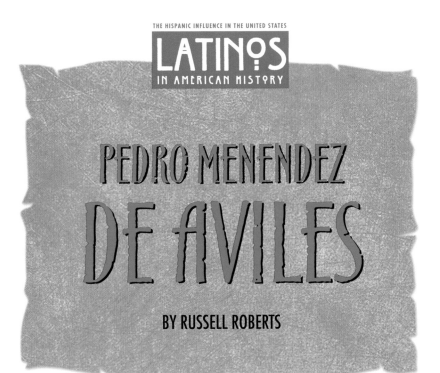

THE HISPANIC INFLUENCE IN THE UNITED STATES

LATIN♀S
IN AMERICAN HISTORY

PEDRO MENENDEZ
DE AVILES

BY RUSSELL ROBERTS

Mitchell Lane
PUBLISHERS

P.O. Box 196
Hockessin, Delaware 19707

THE HISPANIC INFLUENCE IN THE UNITED STATES

LATINOS
IN AMERICAN HISTORY

OTHER TITLES IN THE SERIES

Visit us on the web: www.mitchelllane.com
Comments? email us: mitchelllane@mitchelllane.com

THE HISPANIC INFLUENCE IN THE UNITED STATES

LATINOS
IN AMERICAN HISTORY

PEDRO MENENDEZ
DE AVILES

BY RUSSELL ROBERTS

Printing   2   3   4   5   6   7   8

Library of Congress Cataloging-in-Publication Data

Roberts, Russell, 1953-

Pedro Menéndez De Aviles / Russell Roberts.

p. cm. — (Latinos in American history)

Summary: A biography of the Spanish seaman and explorer who established a colony at St. Augustine and claimed former French lands in Florida for Spain.

Includes bibliographical references (p.) and index.

ISBN 1-58415-150-1 (lib bdg.)

1. Menández de Avilás, Pedro, 1518-1574—Juvenile literature. 2. Explorers—Florida—Biography—Juvenile literature. 3. Explorers—Spain—Biography—Juvenile literature. 4. Florida—History—Spanish colony, 1565-1763—Juvenile literature. [1. Menández de Avilás, Pedro, 1519-1574. 2. Explorers. 3. Florida—History—Spanish colony, 1565-1763] I. Title. II. Series.

E314.M54 R63 2003

975.9'01092—dc21

[B]   2002022145

ABOUT THE AUTHOR: Russell Roberts has written and published books on a variety of subjects, including *Ten Days to a Sharper Memory*, *Discover the Hidden New Jersey*, and *Stolen! A History of Base Stealing*. This is his first book for Mitchell Lane. He lives in Bordentown, New Jersey with his family and a remarkably lazy, yet fiesty calico cat named Rusti.

PHOTO CREDITS: Cover: Northwind Photos; p. 6 Northwind Photos; p. 9 Corbis; p. 10 Corbis; p. 14 The Bridgeman Art Library/Getty; p. 16 Bettmann/Corbis; p. 24 Bettmann/Corbis; p. 26 Corbis; p. 32 Corbis; p. 33 Eye Ubiquitous/Corbis; p. 34 Wolfgang Kaehler/Corbis; p. 38 Archivo Iconografico/Corbis; p. 43 William Bake/Corbis.

PUBLISHER'S NOTE: This story is based on the author's extensive research, which he/she believes to be accurate. Some parts of the text might have been created by the author based on his/her research to illustrate what might have happened years ago, and is solely an aid to readability for young adults.

The spelling of the names in this book follow the generally accepted usage of modern day. The spelling of Spanish names in English has evolved over time with no consistency. Many names have been anglicized and no longer use the accent marks or any Spanish grammar. Others have retained the Spanish grammar. Hence, we refer to Hernando De Soto as "De Soto," but Francisco Vásquez de Coronado as "Coronado." There are other variances as well. Some sources might spell Vásquez as Vazquez. For the most part, we have adapted the more widely recognized spellings.

CONTENTS

CHAPTER 1

CHAPTER 2

CHAPTER 3

CHAPTER 4

CHAPTER 5

CHAPTER 6

Pedro Menéndez de Avilés founded and colonized the city of St. Augustine, Florida for Spain. This illustration, created in the 17th century, shows the colonists laying out the streets. They used string to measure and dug with shovels and pick axes. Much of the information we know about Menéndez comes from an historical account of Gonzalo Solís de Meras, Menéndez's brother-in-law and official recorder of the Menéndez expedition, which survives today.

DEATH ON THE BEACH

CHAPTER 1

Slowly Pedro Menéndez de Avilés, (PAY-droe men-EN-dez day ah-VEE-lace) leader of the Spanish soldiers and settlers who had recently arrived in Florida, strode along the beach. Just a few feet away was the Atlantic Ocean, the surface of its blue-green water sparkling like a hundred tiny diamonds as it reflected the sunlight. The waves rolled gently into shore, the water slapping the sand and then rushing forward, only to stop and then scoot backwards into the ocean again. Overhead Menéndez saw a few birds race across the deep blue sky.

It was a peaceful place, this inlet—surely one of the nicest he had ever seen during his many years in the New World. The shoreline was not usually like this in his native Spain. At home, the shore was often crowded, cluttered with buildings such as the huts of fishermen close to the water, or scarred by dirt roads filled with wagons carrying people coming and going.

But this was different. Although he had been a sailor most of his life and had traveled to many different places in the service of the Spanish crown, particularly for King Philip II, he had rarely seen such natural beauty as this inlet. St. Augustine, the settlement just to the north that he had recently founded, also had an attractive location near the Florida beach.

It would be a shame to spoil this pretty place with the screams of men, and blood and death—but that's just what Menéndez planned to do on this late September day in 1565.

He sighed. His duty was clear. He stopped walking and slowly drew a line in the sand with his long sharp lance. Then he continued on his way.

Right behind him, just a few moments later, came a group of ten French seamen. Their hands were tied behind their backs, and their clothes were torn and tattered. They were being led along the sand by a group of Spanish soldiers. Not far away a much larger group of seamen, about 200 in all, waited anxiously.

The Frenchmen had been sailing to attack St. Augustine when a fearful storm had wrecked their ships. All of them had escaped to shore, but their vessels, which carried all their food, had been destroyed. Once on land, the desperate men had eaten whatever they could find—small animals, fish they had been able to catch, even plants. They were trying to make their way up the coast toward the French settlement of St. Caroline, which lay slightly more than 30 miles to the north of St. Augustine. There, they thought, they would be safe.

But unknown to them, Menéndez had already attacked and captured St. Caroline, killing many of its defenders. When the tired and hungry shipwrecked Frenchmen heard this news, they surrendered to Menéndez. There was no sense trying to make it to a settlement that no longer belonged to them. Now they were prisoners. They had nowhere else to go in this New World.

They hoped that Menéndez would be generous and merciful. He had been generous, giving the hungry men food and drink. Now they would find out about his mercy.

The Spanish soldier in charge of those leading the captured Frenchmen along the beach saw the line in the sand that Menéndez had drawn. He knew what it meant. When the prisoners reached that line, the Spanish fell upon them, attacking them with their swords and lances until not a single prisoner was left alive. When the next group of ten Frenchmen approached the line, they were killed as well. The slaughter continued until all of the French prisoners were dead, except a handful who claimed they were Catholics, like the Spanish. These prisoners were sent to St. Augustine.

Incredibly, about two weeks later, this scene was repeated. The rest of the shipwrecked Frenchmen, including their captain, Jean Ribault, surrendered to Menéndez at the same inlet despite seeing the bodies of their shipmates still lying on the sand and knowing that they might suffer the same fate.

From then on, the once-peaceful inlet was named *Matanzas*—the Place of Slaughters. Pedro Menéndez had ignited an historical controversy that continues to this day.■

This is the Bridge of Lions spanning Matanzas inlet today.

In 1554, Pedro Menéndez de Avilés was named Captain General of the Indies Fleet. In that same year, King Charles V of Spain chose Menéndez as one of the men to take Charles' son (the future Philip II) to England to wed Queen Mary. Menéndez made a name for himself for his daring and bravery.

A LIFE DEVOTED TO THE SEA

Considering his father, it's little wonder that Pedro Menéndez de Avilés was drawn to a life of adventure and service to the Spanish king.

Pedro's father was Juan Alfonso Sánchez de Avilés, who had fought with distinction during the final battles against Spain's Moorish invaders. The Moors had crossed into Spain from North Africa in the eighth century, and the country had been at war ever since. Under King Ferdinand V and Queen Isabella I, the Spanish—including Juan Alfonso—defeated the last remaining Moors in Granada early in 1492. Serving the Spanish monarchy, therefore, was an honored tradition in the family.

Pedro was born as one of the youngest of twenty children on February 15, 1519, in the town of Avilés in the Asturias region on the northern coast of Spain. The area's green hills overlook the shining sea, which beckons to boys and promises escape from ordinary life. Young Pedro excitedly listened to those promises, like a lover who hears his sweetheart whispering pledges of everlasting affection in his ear.

But when Pedro was still a boy his father died. The family was not wealthy, and when his mother, Maria Alonso de Arango, remarried, eight-year-old Pedro was sent to live permanently with a relative. Stubborn, intelligent, and independent, Pedro argued and disagreed with his relative about almost everything. He ran away, and it took six months to find him and bring him back.

When Pedro was still a boy, it was arranged that when he grew up he would marry his ten-year-old cousin, Ana María. Eventually he indeed would marry her, but the youngster had bigger plans in mind right then. He had never stopped listening to the siren call of the sea, and when he was fourteen he ran away again. This time he joined a group of Spanish sailors who were fighting French corsairs, or pirates.

As Menéndez fought the corsairs, he grew into a man. He also developed sailing and military skills that would serve him well throughout his life. At the end of two years he returned home, but not to stay. He planned to sell part of his inheritance from his father and build his own ship. His family and Ana María tried to talk him out of this idea, but his mind was made up. He had fallen under the ocean's spell, and he intended to return to the sea as soon as possible. When the light, fast ship that he ordered built was done, Menéndez went back to sea. Ahead of him lay a life of adventure.

Soon Menéndez was making a name for himself because of his deeds at sea. Some called him little better than a pirate himself, attacking whatever ships he encountered and taking their cargo. Others said that he was a fearless defender of Spain—a brave and daring captain who would risk his life in the service of his country.

He was certainly daring. In one instance, he saw a group of four French ships getting ready to attack a Spanish convoy that contained a bridal party. Although outnumbered four to one, Menéndez attacked the French and succeeded in getting two of them to chase him. When he had put enough distance between his two pursuers, he turned and captured first one, then the other. The other two ships, realizing that they were up against a clever foe, quickly fled.

Victories such as this convinced Spanish King Charles V, and his son—the future Philip II—that Menéndez was a valuable asset to Spain. In fact, in 1554, when Menéndez was 35 years old, he was one of the men chosen to take Philip to England to wed Queen Mary.

That same year, Menéndez was named Captain General of the Fleet of the Indies. It was his duty to protect Spanish ships filled with treasure that were returning from the recently discovered New World. Spain was using the wealth from its new colonies to become a world power. In addition, when Philip became king in 1556 and fought France, he called on Menéndez several times to escort ships and supplies past the hostile French coastline. Menéndez made a name for himself for his daring and bravery.

Once, Menéndez and three squadrons of ships were waiting on the open ocean to escort reinforcement ships when a severe storm blew up. Two of the squadrons fled for shelter, fearful that the storm would sink them. But Menéndez stayed out on the ocean, willing to brave the storm to continue doing his duty. All of his ships survived the rough weather.

Another time, Menéndez was with a large armada of ships out on the open sea when a powerful storm hit. This time, Menéndez ordered all the ships to seek the safety of the nearest harbor. However, it was blocked by a large chain hanging between two buildings that prevented unwanted ships from entering. Without a moment to spare, Menéndez raced ashore and ran to one of the buildings in which a thick, heavy rope was holding the chain. He cut the rope with his sword, allowing all of his ships to crowd into the harbor just as the storm's fury hit. While several ships were sunk, the loss would have been much greater without Menéndez's quick action.

Menéndez was willing to brave storms out on the ocean to continue doing his duty. He was known for his bravery at sea.

In 1559, however, Menéndez became ill with a mysterious fever. The following year, even though he was still not well, Philip again made him Captain General of the Fleet of the Indies. Sick and depressed over the death of his brother Alvaro, Menéndez nevertheless took the assignment, and did so again in 1561. One result was that he became quite wealthy. But even though he was serving his king and his country, Menéndez was making powerful enemies who were jealous of the favor he held with Philip.

These enemies had him arrested and thrown into prison for nearly two years. The charges against him were smuggling, breaking rules, and acting in excess of his orders. Scholars disagree whether the charges were real, or just invented by his rivals. Eventually, even though the charges against him were not proven, Menéndez had to pay a fine.

When he was a free man once more, Menéndez met Philip. The King once again asked him to return to America—but this time he had some new instructions for him.■

Historians believe it was Ponce de Léon, shown in this sketch, who actually claimed Florida for Spain in 1513. De Léon was unable to colonize the area, however. Later in the century, France challenged Spain's claim to Florida, which at that time included most of the southeastern United States. Menéndez was sent back to the New World to colonize Florida and spread Catholicism.

IN THE SERVICE OF A KING— OR A MURDERER?

CHAPTER 3

In 1513 the Spanish explorer Juan Ponce de León had claimed Florida for Spain. Ever since then, Spain had considered Florida as part of its New World empire, which also included much of Central and South America. But even though Ponce and several other explorers had mounted expeditions to Florida, they had been unable to colonize it, primarily because of the resistance of the native populations. In September 1561, after Philip learned of the failure of the most recent expedition, he announced that Spain would no longer try to colonize Florida.

However, France soon became very aggressive about challenging Spain's claim to control Florida. In 1562, an expedition under the command of Jean Ribault explored part of the Florida coast. They discovered the entrance of the St. Johns River—which they called the River Mai—and erected a marble column that claimed this land for France. Two years later another expedition under the leadership of Rene de Laudonnière sailed up the river and established a colony called Fort Caroline, which was only a few miles from modern-day Jacksonville.

These actions outraged many in Spain, including Philip, who considered Florida to be the property of Spain. Something had to be done to cement Spain's dominance in Florida. Otherwise, French ships could use their new base to capture the rich treasure galleons that sailed north along the Florida coast using the powerful current of the Gulf Stream before heading east for Spain.

There was another factor that angered Spain with relation to France's presence in Florida. Many of the French were Lutheran Protestants, while Spain was overwhelmingly Catholic. Religious differences between Catholics and Protestants were very bitter, and often marked by violence. So Spain had another reason to want the French kicked out of Florida—religion.

In Menéndez, Philip saw a tool to both firmly establish Spain's grip on Florida and to deal his hated religious enemies a deadly blow. He named Menéndez as adelantado—the leader and governor—of Florida, and told him to go and colonize the region. At that time, what the Spanish called Florida wasn't just the area of the modern-day state. It consisted of much of what later became the southeastern United States.

Menéndez had other tasks as well. He was directed to chart the waterways in the area to produce guides for other Spanish ships to follow and to sweep the Caribbean clean of any pirates he might find, so that the Spanish treasure ships would be safe. He was given several priests to accompany the expedition in hopes of converting the native inhabitants to the "one true faith"—the Catholic Church. And the King also told Menéndez, a firm believer in the Catholic religion, to exterminate any Lutherans he found in Florida.

Menéndez also had a personal reason for going to Florida. While he was in prison, word had reached him that his son Juan had been shipwrecked near Bermuda. This way, perhaps he could search the area for his lost son.

But just as he was getting ready to depart, word of an ominous development reached the Spanish court. Ribault was preparing an expedition to reinforce the colony that already existed. There was no time to lose.

So in late June 1565, Menéndez left Spain for Florida in ten ships. Besides farm animals such as calves, hogs and sheep, he also took with him soldiers, farmers, priests, and craftsmen such as locksmiths and tanners. He met up with other vessels that were also going to Florida, so that Menéndez was actually in charge of a fleet of more than thirty ships carrying approximately 2600 people.

Menéndez encountered a powerful storm in the middle of the Atlantic. Many of the ships were scattered and others severely damaged. After surviving the storm, Menéndez first stopped at Puerto Rico. From there on August 15 he set sail for Florida with five ships.

On the night of August 27, his small fleet lay becalmed between the Bahama Islands and the coast of Florida. Some of the men wanted to wait for the other ships to show up. But Menéndez disagreed. Every day was important, he believed. So he ordered them forward. Soon afterward, the skies seemed to show that they agreed with him. A huge comet blazed overhead, heading west—toward Florida.

Incredibly, both men arrived in Florida on the same day—August 28, 1565—though they were separated by a little over 100 miles with Ribault at Fort Caroline and

Menéndez landing near modern-day Cape Canaveral. The Spaniards turned northward and continued sailing up the coast. On September 2, the Spaniards met members of the Timucua Indian nation. Using signs, the Indians indicated that the French were even further north.

The next day Menéndez himself met the Timucuas. "They seem to be a noble race," he wrote to Philip.

Then he continued on his way, where he passed "a good harbor with a good beach." On September 4th, Spaniards at last encountered the French, finding four of Ribault's ships anchored just offshore. Their soldiers had already landed, so the ships were undermanned and in no shape for a battle with the Spanish. When Menéndez attacked, the French ships fled. But he couldn't press his advantage because uncharted sandbars near the mouth of the river blocked his ships from going any farther.

Menéndez returned to "the good harbor with the good beach," where some of his other ships had already landed. The chief of the local Timucua village had given them his long house and Menéndez's men were already building fortifications around it.

On September 8, 1565, Menéndez came ashore and officially established his new colony with much celebration. He named it St. Augustine because August 28th, the day when he had first sighted Florida, was St. Augustine's feast day on the Catholic calendar. Drums beat, trumpets blared, flags waved and cannons roared as the curious Native Americans looked on. Then the Spaniards held a Catholic Mass. Finally they served food for everybody, including the Indians. By this act, Menéndez hoped to win the Indians' friendship.

As soon as they finished eating, Menéndez and his men continued to fortify their tiny settlement. So far Menéndez had accomplished one of the tasks King Philip had given him. He had established a colony in Florida. But he still had to deal with the French.

He rightly suspected that a French attack might be imminent. Sure enough, by the first light of dawn three days later, Menéndez looked out to the ocean to see six French ships. Ribault had decided to attack the Spaniards.

However, the French could not get into the harbor to attack the Spanish ships. Now nature took a hand in the drama. A terrible storm hit, and the fierce northeast winds drove the French ships southward, away from St. Augustine. The French were kept busy fighting the storm; they had no time to think about attacking the Spanish.

But attacking the enemy was precisely what Menéndez was thinking about. He knew the storm would keep Ribault away from Fort Caroline for many days, and that the settlement would be extremely vulnerable to an assault during his absence because the men who were on the French ships had obviously been taken from Fort Caroline.

Accordingly, on September 16 Menéndez, with approximately 500 men, set out to march to Fort Caroline. The conditions were terrible; the storm continued with heavy rain soaking the Spanish and their belongings. Some of the soldiers grumbled that Menéndez did not know what he was doing. On the sea he was a master, they said, but on land he was out of his element.

But finally, on September 20, the Spanish approached Fort Caroline. As Menéndez had foreseen, it was lightly defended in Ribault's absence. In addition, the weather had been so bad that the French had been lulled into thinking that an attack was impossible.

Under cover of the weather, Menéndez and his men crept very close to the fort before they launched their assault. The French defenders, under the command of Laudonnière, put up a valiant struggle. But the Spanish were too strong. Out of 242 in Fort Caroline, 132 were killed. The dead may have included women and children, though some sources say that Menéndez ordered them spared. The survivors fled into the surrounding wilderness. Some were able to make their way down to the river's mouth and board two small ships, which carried them back to France.

According to most accounts, the Spanish hanged some Frenchmen from nearby trees, and placed signs over them that read: NOT AS FRENCHMEN, BUT AS LUTHERANS. This would indicate that much of the killing that occurred was sparked by Philip's instructions to exterminate all Lutherans.

Menéndez renamed Fort Caroline San Mateo, and left 300 men to guard it. He then returned to St. Augustine, knowing that the settlement would be in grave danger if Ribault had survived the storm.

A few days later, Menéndez was alerted by Indians that a large group of white men were at an inlet a few miles south of the colony. He knew that these men were almost certainly part of Ribault's fleet who had been shipwrecked by the storm. He went to them and told them that he had captured the French settlement that they were trying to reach. When the Frenchmen heard this, they surrendered. After feeding them, Menéndez had them brought down to the beach and killed in groups of ten, as was described earlier.

Ribault, the French leader, met his end bravely. He observed that if he had been allowed to live he likely would have died within 20 years anyway. "Twenty years more or less were of little account in the life of a man," he said. "From earth we come and to earth we must return."

Within moments he was dead. His memory survives in a Jacksonville high school that bears his name.

Menéndez's chaplain, Francisco Lopez de Mendoza Grajales, wrote a description of the incident that reveals how deeply the two religious factions hated each other.

"As I was a priest, and had bowels of mercy, I begged him (Menéndez) to grant me the favor of sparing those whom we might find to be Christians. He granted it; and I made investigations, and found ten or twelve of the men Roman Catholics, whom we brought back. All the others were executed, because they were Calvinists and enemies of our Holy Catholic faith."

Menéndez shared these feelings. After it was over, he wrote to King Philip, "I had Jean Ribault and all the rest put to the knife, as was necessary for God's service and yours."

When news of these killings reached Europe there was great outrage. Many people felt that Menéndez had killed the Frenchmen unfairly, and called for revenge on the Spaniards. In particular, the relatives of the victims appealed to the French royal court for vengeance in the names of their murdered loved ones.

But no vengeance was immediately forthcoming. The attitude of the French royal court was indifferent, quite possibly because Ribault was a friend and supporter of the French Protestant leader Admiral Gaspard de Coligny, and many were jealous of Coligny's power and influence. If the court acted on behalf of Ribault and his murdered companions, it would seem as if they were supporting Coligny, and he would become even more powerful. In fact, it is highly likely that the warning about Ribault and his mission to Florida was secretly sent to Philip from someone in the French royal court.

Thus no action was taken on behalf of the murdered Frenchmen. Not even a note of protest was sent from France to Spain. It was as if the murders never happened.

Some have called Menéndez a murderer for killing the helpless prisoners. He is often portrayed as an evil butcher and a coward who killed men who could not defend themselves.

But others say there is another side of the story. They say Menéndez did not have enough supplies to feed both the settlers and soldiers at St. Augustine and a large group of prisoners. In addition, the combined French forces, if allowed to regroup, were numerically superior to Menéndez's. It was war, and he had to defeat the enemy and keep his own losses to a minimum. The fact that he did so, contends

Gaspard de Coligny (1517-1572), French admiral and leader of the Huguenots.

this viewpoint, is the mark of a great general and leader, rather than a murderer.

Those who do not condemn Menéndez for the murders add that he was following the orders of his king. Religious violence was quite common at that time, and Menéndez was only doing what Philip had told him to do—exterminate the Lutherans.

Those who feel that Menéndez was not simply a murderer blindly killing his enemies also point to the fact that two months later he found a much smaller group of French castaways who had refused to surrender with the others. They had gone back to the wreckage of their ships, trying to build an escape vessel from the shattered timbers and broken masts lying on the sand. While some of them fled into the jungle at the sight of the Spaniards, many surrendered.

As before, Menéndez fed his prisoners. But this time, instead of killing them, he brought them back to St. Augustine. So there was no killing involved. They apparently were reserved for another fate.

A note in Philip's writing appears on one of the letters that Menéndez sent to the King: "Say to him (Menéndez) that, as to those he has killed, he has done well; and as to those he has saved, they shall be sent to the galleys."

Regardless of the later historical controversy, it is apparent that Menéndez had been very successful in pleasing the man whose approval mattered the most.■

This is a view of St. Augustine, Florida in the mid 1700s. Spain ruled St. Augustine for more than 200 years until the British gained control in 1763. Spain gained control again in 1783 and ruled the settlement until 1821, when Florida became a territory of the United States. During the late 1500s, St. Augustine served as Spain's military headquarters in North America.

THE RAIN MAKER

Whether Menéndez's actions were right or wrong, one thing is certain: the effect of those actions. They effectively ended French influence in Florida. After this, the Spanish controlled Florida for many decades.

But defeating the French was only one part of the puzzle Menéndez had to solve before Florida could be considered colonized for Spain. Even though St. Augustine had been founded, the region was still a vast wilderness which every day presented new obstacles for those living there just to survive.

The difficulties of living in this uncharted land were driven home to Menéndez early in 1566, when he was in Havana. Word arrived that one hundred of the St. Augustine settlers had died. Discouraged at the hardships they had encountered, many of the survivors were ready to abandon Florida and return to Spain.

Menéndez knew that if the colonists were allowed to go back, the survival of the new colony would be threatened.

Immigration from Spain to Florida would virtually cease once the colonists' stories of the difficulties they encountered got out. The entire plan to settle Florida might wither and die.

For Menéndez personally, the prospect of the Florida colonization failing was even riskier. He had already sunk a vast amount of his personal fortune into the venture. If the Florida experiment failed, he would lose all that money. It was plain that St. Augustine needed a strong leader there—a man who had endured hardships in the past and who could boost the colonists' spirits when necessary.

It was plain that St. Augustine needed Menéndez.

But before returning to his colony, he decided to explore the Florida Keys and the southwestern coast of Florida. He had heard that Indians had enslaved Spanish castaways in these regions. Perhaps, he hoped, he might find his son, or at least discover his fate. At the very least, he might be able to rescue some of the castaways. After that, he would continue on to St. Augustine, then head north to found more settlements.

Initially, Menéndez discovered some new deep water ports, with enough water for large ships. But then he found a castaway who said that some of the several hundred other shipwrecked Spaniards were in a town run by a native chieftain named Carlos.

Menéndez decided to invite Carlos aboard his ship under the guise of friendship. Accordingly, the Indian and some of his warriors boarded Menéndez's ship, and the two exchanged gifts, then ate. However, when Carlos tried to leave, Menéndez revealed his true purpose: the rescue of the Spaniards that Carlos held captive.

Looking around, Carlos saw that the time for friendship and easy talk was over. Menéndez had positioned soldiers at key spots around the ship to prevent the Indians from escaping. Seeing that Menéndez was deadly serious, Carlos sent some of his men back to get the Spaniards that they were holding captive.

Soon eight of the captives—the only ones still alive from the scores that been shipwrecked in that region—were on board the Spanish ship.

Shortly thereafter Menéndez visited Carlos. He went to Carlos's village, where the Indian chief reportedly lived in a house so large that it could easily hold two thousand people. Despite the circumstances of their previous meeting, Carlos was happy to see Menéndez. A great celebration followed, the highlight of which was Menéndez speaking to the Indians in their native language. However, the Spaniard was in for a major shock. The woman sitting next to Carlos, who he had assumed to be the Indian's wife and was smiling shyly at him, turned out to be Carlos's sister—who the Indian then gave to Menéndez as his wife.

Menéndez was already married, and as a strict Catholic he knew he couldn't take another wife. But he did not dare to refuse the offer of Carlos's sister for fear of offending the Indians. Thanking his host, Menéndez took his new "bride" back to his ship and turned her over to the Spanish women on board. She was baptized and had her name changed to Antonia, then put aboard another ship in Menéndez's fleet and taken to Havana. There she was given religious instructions.

For his part, Menéndez hurried back to St. Augustine. He arrived there on March 20, 1566 to find the spirits of those at the colony to be very low. The colonists had suffered through a very difficult first winter. Food and medicine were scarce, and besides approximately one hundred who had died, another hundred had fled to the Caribbean.

Therefore, few showed enthusiasm for Menéndez's plan to continue northward and found new settlements. They didn't want to start new towns; they wanted St. Augustine to become better. In fact, yet another hundred colonists deserted to the Caribbean rather than continue living at St. Augustine, or be used to found further settlements.

Menéndez was in a difficult situation. St. Augustine seemed on the verge of collapse, and to make matters worse, San Mateo (the former Fort Caroline) was also struggling with many deaths and desertions. Was Menéndez's Florida dream destined to perish along with the new settlements?

The Spaniard decided to reinforce St. Augustine with 150 of his men, and leave the same number at San Mateo. Although that would seriously deplete his own forces, leaving him with only about 150 men, there was nothing else to do. The two settlements had to be strengthened or they would not survive.

Menéndez and his expedition set off from St. Augustine in late March of 1566. After stopping at San Mateo and dropping off the reinforcements, Menéndez and his depleted crew continued on. Soon they arrived at a harbor off the coast of what is now present-day Georgia.

The local Native American people, who lived in an area called Gaule, came to the shore to meet them. Initially suspicious and hostile, the Indians were soon won over by Menéndez's offer of food and friendship. In communicating with the Indians, he was greatly aided by a shipwrecked Frenchman who was living with the Indians and acted as interpreter.

Menéndez soon learned that the people of Gaule had captured two men from a nearby region known as Orista. They were preparing to sacrifice their captives to the rain gods because no rain had fallen in Gaule for months. As a result, crops had withered and died, and food was scarce in the village.

Here Menéndez saw a chance to convert the Native Americans to the Christian faith, and also to forge the bonds of friendship with the Indians. He asked that the Orista prisoners be turned over to him instead of being sacrificed. He then offered to end the war between the two regions, and said that he would take the captives back to Orista as a peace offering.

Menéndez also indicated that the lack of rain was a punishment from God because of His displeasure over the war and the plans of the people of Gaule to kill their Orista prisoners.

Once Menéndez agreed to leave some of his men in place of the Orista captives, the Indians agreed to let him take their prisoners. He then journeyed to Orista, which was somewhere around the site of present-day Hilton Head, South Carolina. Menéndez met with their leaders and convinced them to make peace with Gaule. The Orista Indians also agreed to become baptized into the Christian faith.

Then Menéndez asked the Orista people to help him select a good location for a settlement. The trust between the two sides was so strong that the Indians gladly did so, and soon Menéndez's men were building a fort at the location. He called it San Felipe, and left another hundred or so men to occupy it.

When Menéndez returned to Gaule, he told of all that had happened there. The village elders of Gaule were hopeful that the events would bring rain, and they told Menéndez how they had been loyal and faithful Christians in his absence.

A little later it did indeed rain—a tremendous downpour that occurred only in the Gaule region. Naturally, the

This painting depicts a street scene in the settlement of St. Augustine, Florida, the oldest permanent settlement established in the United States by Europeans. Note the cross on the church in the painting. Spain wanted to spread Catholicism in the New World.

Indians credited Menéndez for bringing the rain. Word of Menéndez and the miraculous rainfall that he had caused because of his special friendship with God soon spread far and wide. As the Spaniard headed south back to St. Augustine, many Indians paddled their canoes out to meet him. They wanted him to visit their villages and bring his wondrous powers with him. As a result, Menéndez developed a routine of landing at villages, meeting with the Indians, and then erecting a small wooden cross as a symbol of the power of the Christian faith. Undoubtedly, many of the Indians hoped that Menéndez would bring rain to them as well.

It is worth noting that at this time, the Native Americans and Menéndez were friends. He had used his skills at diplomacy to forge bonds of trust and companionship with the Indians he encountered. This was a far different state of affairs than existed in Central and South America, where Spanish cruelties toward the native peoples caused an atmosphere of intense hostility to exist between the two groups.

A 208 ft. high steel cross commemorates the first mass given in America by Father Francisco Lopes de Mendoza Grajales in 1565 at St. Augustine.

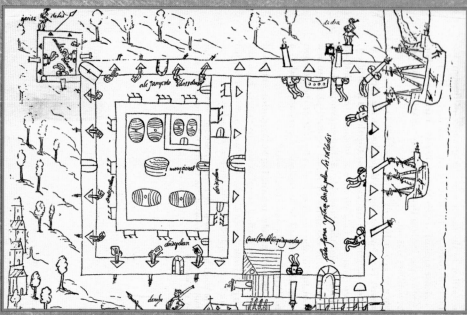

Top: Plan of the Fort at St. Augustine built by Menéndez. The original painting is a crude colored pen and ink sketch drawn in the late sixteenth century.

Bottom: Cannons at Castillo de San Marcos in St. Augustine, Florida shown in the 1990s. It is the oldest masonry fort in the continental United States. Spain began construction in 1672.

THE INDISPENSABLE MAN

Unfortunately for Menéndez, the peaceful relations with the native peoples had vanished by the time he returned to San Mateo. As soon as his ship anchored in the harbor, Menéndez found that the Indians were making war on the Spanish colonizers. He also heard that the wooden fort at St. Augustine had been burned to the ground through the use of fire arrows.

The Spanish had decided that the only way to fight the native Americans was to attack their villages, burn their huts, destroy their canoes, and wreck their crops. The Indians, of course, reacted negatively to this invasion of their villages, and the bad feelings between the two sides had grown.

The Spanish found it virtually impossible to fight the Native Americans. They were used to the European style of warfare, in which columns of crisply marching troops in plain sight faced off against each other. The Spanish weren't used to the type of guerilla warfare practiced by the Indians, in which they hid behind trees and crawled along the ground hidden by high grass.

To make matters worse, the Spanish used a primitive firearm known as an harquebus. While very powerful, the harquebus required a support for shooting, and could only fire after an external match lighted the gunpowder inside it. This entire process took a good deal of time, and the Indians were able to safely watch the Spanish make all the preparations to fire the harquebus. The Indians had learned to anticipate when the gunpowder was about to be lit, and duck away just before the weapon fired.

Menéndez only stayed at San Mateo long enough to collect whatever supplies they could spare for St. Augustine. Unfortunately, the supplies he brought back were not nearly enough, and soon the colony was again suffering from food shortages. Owing to the war with the Indians, no colonist dared go out of the settlement to hunt or fish. Anyone foolhardy enough to attempt that would probably not return alive.

It was decided that Menéndez would make a quick run to Havana for supplies. Once he arrived there, the Spaniard was reunited with Antonia, who was depressed over being away from her native land. Menéndez brought her back with him to Florida, where she was reunited with her brother Carlos.

Menéndez was also pleasantly surprised to discover off the Florida coast one of seventeen ships sent from Spain with 1500 soldiers. He left half of those new men in Florida, at the existing settlements such as St. Augustine. At last, he thought happily, some new colonists to help the tired existing ones survive in the primitive Florida wilderness. Perhaps there was hope for Florida after all.

At this point in his life Menéndez had become the driving force in the struggle to keep the Florida settlements alive. He used his own money to buy supplies for the new settlements, his diplomatic skills to keep peace with the Indians, his persuasiveness to stop the existing colonists from abandoning Florida and returning to Spain, and all of his military training to help keep the new towns safe. Like oxygen, he was vital to the Florida colonists' hopes of survival.

Menéndez spent much of the summer of 1566 journeying up rivers that led into the interior of Florida, meeting with Indian leaders and laying the groundwork of friendship. He was in his late 40s, and had been at sea or away from Spain for most of his adult life. By now he had invested a great deal of time, money and energy in the process of personally meeting with the Native Americans. It is obvious that he was fully committed to the colonization of Florida, and was doing everything that he could to assure that the region was successfully settled.

In August of 1566 he returned to St. Augustine. But, as in the past, he did not linger. He only stayed long enough to help put down another revolt by the colonists against the hardships of frontier life. Then he was once again off, with the feel of a ship's deck beneath his feet. Having given so much attention to Florida, it was finally time to try and accomplish another of King Philip's tasks: clearing the Caribbean of pirates. ■

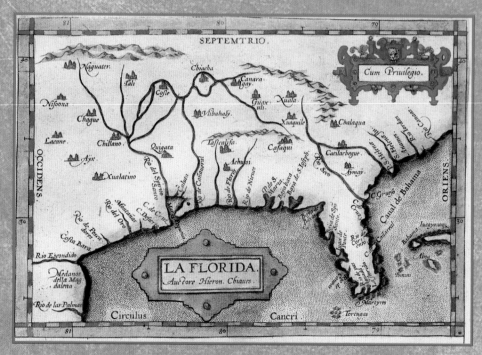

This somewhat inaccurate map of Florida was created by Christopher Plantino in 1588. Notice that what was called Florida was most of the southeastern part of the United States. Some historians believe that "La Florida" was the Spanish term for "North America" at the time.

NEW DUTIES, OLD CONCERNS

B y royal edict, the Spanish cities, towns and ports in the New World had been closed to all foreign vessels. Yet pirate ships from various other nations sailed the waters, robbing and plundering Spanish ships. In addition, when Spanish colonial towns needed supplies, they would not hesitate to trade with any ship they could, be it French, Portuguese, English or Spanish. Many of the pirates considered themselves legitimate merchants and businessmen who just happened to turn to piracy when forced to by economics.

Menéndez assembled a fleet of eight ships and nearly one thousand men to battle the pirates. But aside from strengthening the military and defensive fortifications of such towns as San Juan, Puerto Rico and Havana, Cuba Menéndez and his troops did not see any action in the Caribbean. Even rumors of a large French force bearing down on them turned out to be false.

Once more Menéndez returned to Florida. Indian revolts were again occurring, and he had to use all his diplomatic skills to dampen the fires of rebellion that threatened to overwhelm the Spanish settlements in Florida.

By now Menéndez had been gone too long from Spain. He needed to personally see Philip, to tell him of the destruction of Fort Caroline, the death of Jean Ribault, and of his other adventures in Florida and the Caribbean. He also wanted to impress upon the king how badly the colonists in Florida needed help from Spain in order to survive.

In May 1567, Menéndez left the New World for the Old, setting out for Spain. When he reached it the following month, he held a joyous reunion with his wife Ana María. It was only the fourth time Menéndez had been home in eighteen years.

Then Menéndez went to see King Philip in Madrid, to tell him about the settlements in Florida and how badly they needed greater assistance from Spain. By now there were seven settlements in all: San Mateo, St. Augustine, Santa Lucía, and Tequesta on the eastern coast, Tocobaga and San Antón on Florida's western coast, and Santa Elena, on the coast of present-day South Carolina.

Philip listened carefully to Menéndez. The King was particularly intrigued by Menéndez's belief that Chesapeake Bay, which he had visited, was the legendary Northwest Passage, a direct route from the Atlantic Ocean to the Pacific Ocean and the riches of the Orient.

The King was extremely impressed by all that Menéndez had accomplished. He created a new title and awarded it to Menéndez: Captain General of the West. Then in January 1568 came a further honor. Menéndez was given the Commandery of the Holy Cross of Zarza—a tremendous honor.

But then bad news from Florida began to arrive. Indian uprisings were occurring at many of the settlements that had been founded. Early in 1568, his nephew, Pedro Menéndez Marquez, commanded three ships that visited the settlement at Tocobaga. He found two dead Spanish soldiers. Learning that Indians had killed everyone else, he burned the village.

Even worse, San Mateo—the former French Fort Caroline—was destroyed later that year. A private French force had traveled to Florida determined to take revenge for the killing of Ribault and the others. Its leader was the Chevalier Dominic de Gourges, who had been captured by the Spaniards and forced to serve under conditions of virtual slavery by rowing in Spanish galleys. Once in Florida de Gourges had made an alliance with the Indians, who by now hated the Spaniards as much as he did after his harsh treatment as a captive. Together the twin forces had overwhelmed San Mateo. Some Spaniards had been hanged with an inscription burned into the wood over their heads, just as Menéndez had done earlier with the French. This one read: NOT AS SPANIARDS AND MARINERS, BUT AS TRAITORS, ROBBERS, AND MURDERERS.

Fearing the collapse of everything he had worked for in the New World, Menéndez hastened back to Havana, arriving there in late summer. The Spanish colonies were hanging on by a thread.

Menéndez did what he could to help the Florida colonies, but along with the honors Philip had given him had come other duties, and he had to keep returning to Spain. He could not devote the concentrated effort to Florida that it needed. By September 1569, despite the worsening conditions in Florida, Menéndez was back in Spain. He left Spain again for Florida in the early part of 1570, but was back in Spain by December of that same year. Philip gave him permission to recruit 100 more farmers for Florida, as well as supplies and other necessities, and Menéndez spent several months assembling his little expedition. It finally sailed in May 1571.

However, no sooner did he arrive in the New World than he had to make arrangements to convoy and protect ships filled with treasure back to Spain.

Besides the bad news from Florida, Menéndez also heard that a group of Christian missionaries he had authorized to settle a colony along the Chesapeake Bay had all been killed. Swiftly he traveled to the Chesapeake to try and find some definitive word about the missionaries' fate.

He arrived back at St. Augustine in December, yet he did not stay long. He immediately made plans to return to Havana. The colonists there needed him as well, and he figured that he could pick up supplies for the Florida settlements. Although he was shipwrecked just below St. Augustine, he and all of his crew managed to find their way back to the settlement just in time to help fight off an attack on the colony by English ships. Little did he suspect that this visit to the first colony he had founded would be his last.

Again Menéndez went to the Caribbean, only to return once more to Spain in the summer of 1572. Incredibly, he was doing all of this traveling back and forth by sailing ship, yet maintaining a grueling pace that would leave a modern jet-setter weary with fatigue.

But this time when he came home to Spain he returned for good. Never again would he leave for Florida, as duties for Philip kept him almost constantly busy in Spain for the rest of his life. Yet the New World was never far from his thoughts. He tried to manage affairs there from Spain, even though he was thousands of miles away. But there was no substitute for being there in person. On September 7, 1574, he wrote that "After the salvation of my soul, there is nothing in this world I want more than to be in Florida."

Soon after writing those words, a fever struck Menéndez. He was 55 years old, had been in service to King Philip for nearly twenty years, and at sea far longer than that. He was tired and weary from the many responsibilities that he held, and from the constant voyaging from place to place.

There is no way to know what his thoughts were as the fever closed in on him. It is likely that he thought about Florida—its white sand beaches, its many rivers teeming with fish and its thick jungles alive with Native Americans and wildlife. He had devoted years of his life trying to carve a civilization out of its wilderness.

Pedro Menéndez de Avilés died on September 17, 1574.

And something else died at the same time: the Spanish desire to conquer more colonies in Florida by the sword. Just before Menéndez died, King Philip issued three sets of laws that stipulated that any future expansion would come under the direction of the Catholic Church, not explorers such as Menéndez.

Although an era died with him, the settlement he founded—St. Augustine—would go on to become the oldest city in the United States. It would not only survive, but grow and prosper over the years—a monument to its founder's strength and courage. ■

Colorful creeping flowers surround a window of shops on Charlotte Street in St. Augustine, Florida. The narrow streets and Spanish-style architecture of St. Augustine reflect the city's rich history.

CHRONOLOGY

1519   born on February 15 in Avilés

1527   goes to live with a relative

1554   escorts Philip, then the heir to the Spanish throne, to England to marry Queen Mary

1554   named Captain General of the Fleet of the Indies for the first time

1563   is arrested and imprisoned for nearly two years

1565   named adelantado (leader and governor) of Florida

1565   founds St. Augustine on September 8

1565   captures Fort Caroline, kills Jean Ribault and other Frenchmen

1566   "brings rain" to Gaule

1567   returns to Spain

1567   named Captain General of the West

1568   receives the Commandery of the Holy Cross of Zarza

1568   San Mateo destroyed

1574   dies at age 55

TIMELINE IN FLORIDA HISTORY

1492   Moors are driven from Granada, their final foothold in Spain

1492   Christopher Columbus discovers the New World

1506   Columbus dies

1513   Juan Ponce De León becomes the first European to land in Florida

1513   Vasco de Nuñez de Balboa crosses Isthmus of Panama and becomes first European to view Pacific Ocean

1521   Ponce De León returns to found a settlement on the Gulf Coast, but is mortally wounded by Native Americans

1526   Lucas Vázquez de Ayllon tries to found colony on the South Carolina coast with 600 men, women and children

1528   Panfilo de Narváez lands in Florida to try to start a colony

1531   Francisco Pizarro begins conquest of Peru

1539   Hernando de Soto comes to the Gulf Coast of Florida looking for gold

1540   Francisco Vázquez de Coronado begins an exploration of the Southwest that eventually extends as far as modern-day Kansas

1559   Tristan de Luna y Arellano leads a large expedition from Mexico to try to found a colony in Florida

1561   Discouraged by failures to found a colony in Florida, King Philip II announces that Spain will no longer pursue settlements there

1564   French under leadership of Jean Ribault found colony at mouth of St. John's River near present-day Jacksonville

1565   Pedro Menéndez de Avilés founds St. Augustine and massacres French colonists in Florida

1586   English privateer Francis Drake burns St. Augustine, but its inhabitants quickly rebuild the settlement

1607 Jamestown colony founded

1620 Pilgrims land at Plymouth Rock

1698 Pensacola founded

1763 Great Britain receives Florida from Spain as a result of winning the French and Indian War

1775–1783 Florida colonists remain loyal to Great Britain during the Revolutionary War

1783 Great Britain returns Florida to Spain as a result of losing the Revolutionary War

1810 U.S. settlers in western Florida rebel and declare the Republic of West Florida

1817-1818 First Seminole War

1819 Spain sells Florida to the United States

1835-1842 Second Seminole War

1845 Florida becomes a state

FOR FURTHER READING

Doherty, Kieran. *Soldiers, Cavaliers, and Planters: Settlers of the Southeastern Colonies*. Minneapolis, MN: Oliver Press, 1999.

Lyon, Eugene. *Enterprise of Florida: Pedro Menéndez de Avilés and the Spanish Conquest of 1565-1568*. Gainesville, FL: University of Florida Press, 1976.

Manucy, Albert. *Menéndez*. Sarasota, FL: Pineapple Press, Inc., 1992.

Solis de Meras, Gonzalo. *Pedro Menendez de Aviles: Memorial*. Gainesville, FL: University of Florida Press, 1964.

Thompson, Kathleen. *Pedro Menéndez De Avilés*. Milwaukee, WI: Raintree Publishers, 1990.

ON THE WEB

http://www.publicbookshelf.o...html/Our_Country_Vol_1/
pedromene_ci.html

http://www.bama.ua.edu/prest003/pedro.html

http://www.floridahistory.org/floridians

http://www.hispaniconline.com/hh/us_ltn_presence2.html

http://www.fordham.edu/halsall/mod/1565staugustine.html

GLOSSARY

Armada (ar-MA-da) a large force of ships

Calvinist (KAL-vi-nist) another name for a Protestant

Corsair (KOR-sair) a pirate

Convoy (KON-voi) a number of ships grouped together

Exterminate (ik--STUR-me-nate) destroy totally; get rid of

Galleon (GAL-ee-on) a large sailing vessel

Galley (GAL-ee) ship that uses massive oars, often pulled by slaves, to
move through the water

Indifferent (in-DIFF-er-ent) without interest or concern

Inheritance (in-HER-I-tens) to take or receive by succession as an heir

Interpreter (in-TUR-PRET-er) person who translates from one language to another

Lance (LANS) a long weapon with a metal head

Maroon (ma-ROON) to put ashore and leave on a desolate island or
coast

Missionaries (MISH-uh-nar-ees) a group of people sent to a newly
settled land to carry on religious, educational, or medical work

Squadron (SKWOD-ren) A specific unit that is part of a larger group

INDEX